Thirsty

Thirsty

Encouragement for Moments of Difficulty

MAYA LOGO

RESOURCE *Publications* • Eugene, Oregon

THIRSTY
Encouragement for Moments of Difficulty

Copyright © 2024 Maya Logo. All rights reserved. Except for brief quotations in critical publications or reviews, no part of this book may be reproduced in any manner without prior written permission from the publisher. Write: Permissions, Wipf and Stock Publishers, 199 W. 8th Ave., Suite 3, Eugene, OR 97401.

Resource Publications
An Imprint of Wipf and Stock Publishers
199 W. 8th Ave., Suite 3
Eugene, OR 97401

www.wipfandstock.com

PAPERBACK ISBN: 979-8-3852-2729-7
HARDCOVER ISBN: 979-8-3852-2730-3
EBOOK ISBN: 979-8-3852-2731-0

07/16/24

To all those who have experienced suffering, had that suffering minimized, and were denied the space to heal. God sees you; he does not want that suffering to continue. Repressing it only encourages it to take root within and effect every area of your life. The bible shares that he has no plan to harm you. His only plan is to prosper you. Prosperity simply means growth, to flourish. He wants you to experience growth and advancement in every area of your life. The suffering is hard but not intended to be permanent. It is a precursor to the best that is always in front of you.

Praying for your best,
Maya

True unity is the product of mutual respect,
mutual purpose and mutual passion.

MONDAY

Mirror

You're above the skies, you made the seas
Beyond land and earth, you reign supreme
Yet you've chosen to set your heart on me
I've been claimed, completely set free

Who am I but your child
Purchase of your sacrifice
In your majesty wonder envelops me
By your blood justified
Partaker of new life

Don't need approval from the world
Your crimson flow confirmed my worth
Carefully designed before my birth
Irrevocable bond more than I deserve

Who am I but your child
Purchase of your sacrifice
In your majesty wonder envelops me
By your blood justified
Partaker of new life

Monday

Never knew love but I'm convinced
Assured by your promise from within
Nothing can separate
You overcame all hate

Who am I but your child
Purchase of your sacrifice
In your majesty wonder envelops me
By your blood justified
Partaker of new life

Prayer: Father, thank you for embracing me as yours. Help me to hold onto that truth when I am rejected, unaccepted, or unappreciated. Let your love flow through and to me.

Action Response Plan:

In response to this truth, I will . . .

_____
_____
_____
_____
_____

TUESDAY

Psalm 27

Though a mob rise against
I will rest, I will not fear
Though they scheme and they test
I find confidence because you're near
One thing, one thing, anchors me
It sets me free
Lifted up with enemies all around
My song rises and my praises resound

Hallelujah to the great I am
I'm holding nothing back
Hallelujah, Hallelujah
Hallelujah, Hallelujah
Hallelujah, Hallelujah
Hallelujah
Hallelujah

Though trouble multiplies
Darkness won't eclipse your light
Though many strive and I struggle

Tuesday

I'll reach for you, my faith won't crumble
One thing, one thing, anchors me
It sets me free
Lifted up with enemies all around
My song rises and my praises resound

Hallelujah to the great I am
I'm holding nothing back
Hallelujah, Hallelujah
Hallelujah, Hallelujah
Hallelujah, Hallelujah
Hallelujah
Hallelujah

Prayer: Father, I praise you for who you are. When I face challenges, I know that you are near and that you care. Help me to hold onto that truth when I am rejected, unaccepted, or unappreciated. Let your love flow through and to me.

Action Response Plan:

In response to this truth, I will . . .

_____
_____
_____
_____
_____

WEDNESDAY

He calls him Peter, his rock. I am sure that was a shock to Peter. Nothing in his actions showed the fortitude and stability of a rock. But Jesus reminds Peter to rise up from his failure after it happens and get back to his purpose. The act of falling did not overshadow Peter's identity. Who he was, was not synonymous with what he did. Jesus knew that, but Peter had to learn to separate his failure from who he was. He had to distance himself from what happened. Is there something that is holding you back from being who God created you to be? Are there weights that are trying to keep you from rising to the new life God has for you? God's forgiveness and restoration is more powerful than anyone's word or anything that you could do. Peter is asked to face his past and make a choice. Jesus tells Peter that love means leaving the past behind and living in the fullness of his new life. What do you choose? You can leave the past in the past and walk in your present with purpose. Let the light of the world be the beacon that leads you to fulfill God's purpose in your life.

Prayer: Father, I am so grateful that you see beyond my failures. Thank you for creating me with a specific purpose and design. Help me to hold on to the worth you give me and live like I am meant to be loved.

WEDNESDAY

Action Response Plan:

In response to this truth, I will . . .

_____
_____
_____
_____
_____

THURSDAY

"We should have never hoped for more," the people cried. The temptation to return to slavery was strong. Slavery was not easy but familiar. They knew how to manage under the oppression despite being diminished by it. A story that moves from an experience of being abused to another experience of being abused creates a tendency to wander back to more of the same; especially when things are unfamiliar. What they were facing deprived them of any and all control over their circumstances. They were forced to be completely reliant on God.

In the midst of all the looming chaos God reminds them that the story does not end there. They were not destined to stay trapped between their oppressors and obstacles to the promise. Neither are you. Hope and new life are within reach.

Prayer: Father, you are so kind and caring. You understand when I need you. You know when I am overwhelmed. Help me to trust you and be willing to see beyond the pain, hurt, the familiar or the comfortable. Let your love flow through and to me.

Action Response Plan:

In response to this truth, I will . . .

_____
_____
_____
_____
_____

FRIDAY

On the Cross

He could barely hear their verbal assaults as he pulled air into his collapsing lungs. "Cursed by God" was one of many jeers that rose from the hateful crowd. Yet, in the middle of this piercing darkness he secured God's unwavering approval and his greatest triumph. He moved that much closer to resurrection.

Prayer: Father, your word and plans are unchanging. Your plans are for my good and your purpose. Remind me of the bigger picture when the weight of the moment becomes too heavy. Let your love flow through and to me.

Action Response Plan:

In response to this truth, I will . . .

_____
_____
_____
_____
_____

SATURDAY

> 28 When they heard this, the people in the synagogue were furious. 29 Jumping up, they mobbed him and forced him to the edge of the hill on which the town was built. They intended to push him over the cliff, 30 but he passed right through the crowd and went on his way.
> Luke 4: 28-30 (NLT)

THE PEOPLE REJECTED AND berated Jesus. He responded with a simple truth. He told them their unwillingness to accept him kept them from receiving what he had to offer. That meant they lost the opportunity to be healed, delivered, restored, and strengthened. They lost everlasting life. Jesus never denied them his service and never denied his identity.

He stayed true to himself despite their awful actions. We too have to remain true to our new nature as believers. There is no need to mirror the behavior of our attackers. The choice to keep your character is what makes the difference between being pushed to the edge and being pushed over it.

Jesus was pushed to the edge by the mob. They had him right at the cliff. But he walked through the crowd and headed back to fulfilling his purpose. So we can train ourselves to be unwavering in our commitment to our purpose. When pushed to the edge we won't be shoved over, we will have the strength to walk away.

Prayer: Father, I am so grateful that you meet us at our point of need. There is no pain too great for you to heal and absolutely nothing that can keep us from protection found in your love.

Encourage us in our brokenness. Let the reality of heaven fill our field of vision.

Action Response Plan:

In response to this truth, I will . . .

_____
_____
_____
_____
_____

Action Response Review

How have my plans or perspective changed my experience this week?

_____
_____
_____
_____
_____

MONDAY

Stephen was surrounded. The yelling from the crowd grew to a deafening pitch. Suddenly a rock sailed through the air. The pain, on impact, coursed through is body; only to be repeated by another and another. He would have fallen under the intensity of the assault if he had not just experienced something more intense. He looked up and saw the clouds part like a curtain. The memory helped him tune out the angry mob. He saw Jesus sitting on his throne to the right of the Father. The account of Stephen's experience in Acts offers us a glimpse of heaven's reality. It extends beyond the shadow of pain. The hardships, false accusations, betrayal and malicious acts that affect us so deeply are products of shadows and darkness. God's light is greater than what we experience in shadow living. It is so great that it can carry us through our pain. It can shield us in the storm and propel us into God's presence. We can find refuge there.

Prayer: Father, you know everything we suffer and will suffer in this life. There is nothing we will ever experience that you have not prepared a way for us to endure. Help us to see as you see. Help us to feel you near and experience your tangible presence through hardships. Let the reality of heaven fill our field of vision.

MONDAY

Action Response Plan:

In response to this truth, I will . . .

_____
_____
_____
_____
_____
_____

TUESDAY

Times of difficulty and challenge are part of the human experience. While exemption from hardship seems appealing, the bible suggests that type of existence would be harmful to us. In the absence of suffering, we would lose the opportunity for growth. We would have a shallow understanding of love and lack depth of character. In the bible (John 11) we learn that there is a family that Jesus loves deeply. In fact, because of his great love for Lazarus' family he allows Lazarus to die and his sisters to experience profound sorrow and despair. He is compelled to that course of action because of his love and foresight. There is a bigger picture. He knows that beyond the suffering there is joy and growth that are a direct result of that hardship. It is tempting to focus on the depth of the present pain and become consumed by the moment. But God promises that on the other side of the pain, in the moments that follow, there is joy for sorrow. There is hope for tomorrow, wisdom and strength to endure. That remains true for you. Better is still within reach.

Prayer: Father, we know that you are above all things and beside us in all things. The pain and hardships of life can be so intense. Thank you for comforting me in my pain. Help me to trust that this is not the end of my story. Remind me that you are working everything together for my good and your glory.

Tuesday

Action Response Plan:

In response to this truth, I will . . .

_____
_____
_____
_____
_____

WEDNESDAY

We will not be shattered or be shaken.
No matter what the enemy has taken.
The darkness tries to swallow the light.
But in our hearts hope's still burning bright.
We will not be shaken; we are rooted in the truth.
We will not be shaken; God protected, shatterproof

Prayer: Father, I am so grateful that you are the source of my hope and strength. Thank you for encouraging me when it feels like my world is falling apart. Help me to remain confident in you. Let your presence be even more tangible to me right now.

Action Response Plan:

In response to this truth, I will . . .

_____
_____
_____
_____

THURSDAY

> We didn't forget you or turn away from you. But still hard times came, opposition rose up even while our hearts stayed faithful (based on Psalm 44:17–18).

THAT SENTIMENT WAS EXPRESSED by people who knew their hardships were not some form of punishment. The truth is, life is rife with challenges. They are there irrespective of the choices you make. Jesus advised us to anticipate the trouble and understand its purpose. His specific words were, "I have told you these things so that in me you might have peace. In this world you will have trouble. But take heart, I have overcome the world" (John 16:33). Something about knowing the truth and having the right perspective decreases trouble's sting. It shields your heart and fortifies you. Next time the sharp edges of life threaten to shred your peace, let God's truth shield you and dull the impact.

Prayer: Father, the depth of your love is beyond me. Thank you for knowing my needs before I do. You prepared for every circumstance I could ever face. Help me to practice trust as a discipline and hold onto your peace in the midst of trouble.

THURSDAY

Action Response Plan:

In response to this truth, I will . . .

_____
_____
_____
_____
_____

FRIDAY

Grief and uncertainty crowded his thoughts. Moses, his mentor, was dead and an entire group of families were looking to him for their next move. His thoughts churned as he stood in the blazing sun. So he quieted himself. It was clear that the only possible direction was forward. The body of water in their way could not stop their progress. If he chose to agree God would open the path. Too bad the path would not open first. That is how it is with faith. First you cross the valley of indecision and only then the way is made to take the next steps in your journey. Joshua knew this all too well. Natural logic and self-preservation are often in conflict with faith reasoning. Thankfully, God understands. He prepared Joshua and encouraged him. He told him, "I am with you just as much as I was with Moses" (Joshua 3:7). Jesus repeats that reminder for us, "and you can be sure, I am always with you, even to the very end" (Matt 28:20, NIrV). It's okay to make the choice to leave indecision behind. Once you do, watch your path unfold.

Prayer: Father, I am so grateful that you understand the limits of my understanding. Thank you for being compassionate with me when I hesitate or feel unsure of my next step. Help me to lean on you for direction and move forward in time with you.

FRIDAY

Action Response Plan:

In response to this truth, I will . . .

_____
_____
_____
_____
_____

SATURDAY

Fully rejected while fully embraced
Fueled by promise, belonging through grace

THERE ARE TIMES WHEN we feel like we are relegated to the side lines. We are not chosen for the team, the job, the club. Those moments can make us question whether we will ever find a place of acceptance. This is especially true in situations when our will or person has been violated. There is a place for you where no one can ever deny your access. It is in God's family. Once you accept Jesus, he says there is nothing that can snatch you from his hand. You are caught in the grip of his grace. He chose you and plans for you to prosper.

Prayer: Father, I am so grateful that you see beyond my failures. Thank you for creating me with a specific purpose and design. Help me to hold on to the worth you give me and put it to good use. Let your love flow through and to me.

Action Response Plan:

In response to this truth, I will . . .

_____
_____
_____
_____
_____

SATURDAY

Action Response Review

How have my plans or perspective changed my experience this week?

_____
_____
_____
_____
_____

MONDAY

Jesus came to shift our world view. He offers us a new perspective from which we can evaluate ourselves and the world around us. We are then called to live from that new place of understanding. There is great freedom that comes from being able to see without distortions. You are free to stop letting others weigh you down with their judgements against you. You are free to forgive those who lied about you, falsely accused you. You are free to stop letting the sins of others distort you. Take your freedom and live.

Jesus Heals a Blind Man Mark 8:22–26 (NLT)

> 22 When they arrived at Bethsaida, some people brought a blind man to Jesus, and they begged him to touch the man and heal him. 23 Jesus took the blind man by the hand and led him out of the village. Then, spitting on the man's eyes, he laid his hands on him and asked, "Can you see..."

Prayer: Father, I am so grateful for your loving kindness. Thank you for giving me the opportunity to experience your best and be my best self. Help me to release and leave anything or anyone who keeps me from maturing and living my best. Let your wisdom and clarity guide my choices.

Monday

Action Response Plan:

In response to this truth, I will . . .

_____
_____
_____
_____
_____

TUESDAY

> The air was hot, still, and dry. There had not been any rain for a very long time. But the whisper of wind dancing across his face assured him things were about to change. He looked toward the clear blue sky, uttering a heartfelt prayer, and watched for rain. After several long, agonizing moments a small cloud moved in.
> (1 Kings 18:4–46)

IT IS ALWAYS HARD when you are waiting for God to fulfill a promise or for an answer to prayer. In spite of our uncertainty and discomfort persistence is crucial. Jesus advises us to continually pray and never abandon hope (Luke 11:1–15, 18:1–8). Nothing God promised will fail to be manifested. He only asks us to keep watching, praying and seeking. The promise will never disappoint.

Prayer: Father, I am so grateful that you are always at work. Thank you for inviting me to join you in your work. Help me to remain focused and committed to that work. Let the knowledge of who you are consistently be in front of me.

Action Response Plan:

In response to this truth, I will . . .

_____
_____
_____
_____

WEDNESDAY

THERE ARE CIRCUMSTANCES THAT do not align with our expectations. They challenge our preconceived notions and unsettle us. Jesus reassures us that circumstances are temporary. They are used to fulfill a greater purpose in God's greater plan. Don't get distracted by the difficulty. Determine how the difficulty is positioning you for God's greater purpose.

> "You planned to harm me. But God planned it for good. He planned to do what is being done. He wanted to save many lives." Genesis 50:20 NIrV

Prayer: Father, I am so grateful that you know how everything works together in my life. Thank you for reassuring me that all difficulties serve a specific purpose. Help me to remember that they will ultimately work for my good. Let your truth anchor me.

Action Response Plan:

In response to this truth, I will . . .

_____
_____
_____
_____

THURSDAY

Jesus Heals a Blind Man

22 When they arrived at Bethsaida, some people brought a blind man to Jesus, and they begged him to touch the man and heal him. 23 Jesus took the blind man by the hand and led him out of the village. Then, spitting on the man's eyes, he laid his hands on him and asked, "Can you see?" 24 The man looked around. "Yes," he said, "I see people, but I can't see them very clearly. They look like trees walking around." 25 Then Jesus placed his hands on the man's eyes again, and his eyes were opened. His sight was completely restored, and he could see everything clearly. 26 Jesus sent him away, saying, "Don't go back into the village on your way home."
Mark 8:22–26 NLT

THE BLIND MAN HEALED by Jesus no longer saw men as trees. He saw things for what they were and could interact with them appropriately. The blind man was told not to go back where he was before he gained his sight. There was something about the place or people that contributed to his blindness. The man is called to make a break with those associations. When you are used to spark evolution there will be an initial phase of struggle. The struggle may be within and without. In the end, accepting your sight makes everyone and everything better.

Thursday

Prayer: Father, I am so grateful that you are able to heal me. Thank you that no experience is wasted or worthless. Help me to see as you see and maximize every opportunity.

Action Response Plan:

In response to this truth, I will . . .

_____
_____
_____
_____
_____

FRIDAY

THERE IS NO WORK that God starts but fails to complete. He said he will finish the work he started in you. So be encouraged. In the words of David:

> "Take charge! Take heart! Don't be anxious or get discouraged. God, my God, is with you in this; he won't walk off and leave you in the lurch. He's at your side until every last detail is completed for conducting the worship of God" (1Chronicles 28:20, MSG).

David was talking to his son about a job he had to do. You have a job to do also. Renew your mind as many times as it takes. Repeat what Jesus said to Jairus. Keep rehearsing it, "don't be afraid, just have faith." God will fulfill his purpose in your life! Things are not always what they seem. Don't be afraid, only believe.

Prayer: Father, I am so grateful that you have a plan for my life. Thank you for committing yourself to completing the work you started in me. Help me to trust your plan. Let your promise encourage me.

FRIDAY

Action Response Plan:

In response to this truth, I will . . .

_____
_____
_____
_____
_____

SATURDAY

THE WALLS OF HIS city were in ruins. So he set his mind to rebuild. As he began the process his opponents came to destroy his work and rob his hope. They did not like what he was working toward. It was not so much the work he was doing in that moment. It was what the work implied. It was what the work would inspire and produce. He was building hope, courage, and faith. This is an excerpt from his story:

> When Sanballat heard that we were rebuilding the wall he exploded in anger, vilifying the Jews. In the company of his Samaritan cronies and military he let loose: "What are these miserable Jews doing? Do they think they can get everything back to normal overnight? Make building stones out of make-believe? (Nehemiah 4:1–2, MSG)"

His enemies did not want the disheartened, oppressed, dejected people of Israel to get any ideas. They did not want them to believe again. They did not want them to remember their worth and purpose. So they fought Nehemiah on every front. They called him names, slandered him, plotted to kill him, put obstacles in his way, threatened him, tried to seed confusion, and worked to sabotage his efforts.

Nehemiah was rebuilding a physical place. We are rebuilding our lives. We are more than our limitations, more than our circumstances. Life is about more than being accepted. It reminds us when we go through rivers of difficulty and the fire of oppression that we can thrive. Stay armed with truth and determined. The weapons of our warfare are not physical but they are powerful for destroying great opposition. Do not live in the limits of others' projections. Keep working and moving in and toward your purpose.

Prayer: Father, I am so grateful that you are with me in the face of oppression and hardship. Thank you for preparing me to face these challenges. Help me to rehearse the truth and exercise the skills you are teaching me.

Action Response Plan:

In response to this truth, I will . . .

_____
_____
_____
_____
_____

Action Response Review

How have my plans or perspective changed my experience this week?

_____
_____
_____
_____
_____

BONUS DEVOTION

She had done it. There was no denying it. The crowd roared, threatening her with violence because of it. They brought it and her to be judged. Fury and disgust burned in their eyes. Their hands were ready with stones. They motioned the judge to take action. She breathed sparingly, expecting the end at any moment. Much to her surprise what she heard was not a judgment against her. It was a passionate declaration of her pardon. Jesus forgave her sin.

God sees and separates who you are from what you do. It does not matter if it is sexual sin, greed, gossip, stealing, the list could go on. If you have found yourself buried under the weight of your own sin and/or the sins of others' accusations/actions know that Christ came to set you free. You are free to stop doing what is contrary to who you truly are, as a vessel of honor. You are free to stop letting others weigh you down with their judgements against you.

You are free to forgive those who lied and falsely accused you. You are free to stop sinning and free to stop letting the sins of others distort you. Take your freedom and live.

Prayer: Father, I am so grateful that you know the depth of our pain. Thank you for calling us children of great worth. Help me to let go of the weights I allow people to place on me that distort my image.

BONUS DEVOTION

Action Response Plan:

In response to this truth, I will . . .

_____
_____
_____
_____
_____

BONUS DEVOTION

People can manipulate us into shifting our focus and engaging in unproductive activities and thinking. Religious leaders of Jesus' time did their best to derail and discredit him. Using the pretense of concern for the law, they attempted to lure him into needless debate. "They said this, testing him, that they might have some reason to accuse him. But Jesus stooped down and wrote on the ground with his finger, as though he did not hear them." John 8:6

Jesus did not take the bait. In fact, if his clear act of ignoring them once was not enough, he persisted in ignoring them making it clear that his activity in the moment was his primary focus.

> "And again, he stooped down and wrote on the ground."
> John 8:8

It is important that we take time to respond and avoid reacting. Responding gives us the grace to decide how to exercise our power. Selective inattention may seem like a lack of response. However, it is the loudest answer we can give to manipulation or covert maliciousness. Maintain your focus, retain your power.

Prayer: Father, I am so grateful that your presence can overpower the distractions that vie for our attention. Thank you that we do not need to perform or earn your approval. Help me to stay grounded in your love and purpose for my life.

BONUS DEVOTION

Action Response Plan:

In response to this truth, I will . . .

_____
_____
_____
_____
_____

www.ingramcontent.com/pod-product-compliance
Lightning Source LLC
Chambersburg PA
CBHW071405160426
42813CB00084B/532